The Salt Harvest

for my mother,
Eileen Walls

The Salt Harvest
Eoghan Walls

SEREN

Seren is the book imprint of
Poetry Wales Press Ltd.
57 Nolton Street, Bridgend, Wales, CF31 3AE
www.serenbooks.com

The right of Eoghan Walls to be identified as
the author of this work has been asserted in accordance
with the Copyright, Designs and Patents Act, 1988.

ISBN: 978-1-85411-549-2

A CIP record for this title is available from the British Library.

The publisher acknowledges the financial assistance of the Welsh Books Council.

Cover photograph: Rhossili (detail) © Aled Rhys Hughes
www.aledrhyshughes.co.uk

Printed in Bembo by The Berforts Group Ltd, Stevenage

Contents

Cockles

Take the orange meat into your muscled spaces.
Five years they filtered sewage on Morecambe flats,
nestled as dense as teeth against strong tidal scrapes,

counting the oilspills until Yu Hui slapped his plank
and bore them up by griddle and craam in the early stars,
Yu Hui who ended in sand as wind blasted North off the map,

stilling the tubes of his *cochleae cordis*. Tear them apart,
boiled in cream and crushed with garlic on your sideplate,
alive oh, to feed the crusted bivalves of your heart.

Terminal One

The trees are uprooted between the eye and the horizon,
to still the birdlife. The border markers of the zone
are hung instead with windsocks and a steady drone

declaring the wind as the new rule of this geography,
the earth offering only a muddy reflection of the sky
that sustains nothing. Or little more than nothing. Only

a few trucks and low buildings on either side of a road
that starts in grass and ends with nowhere else to go.
This is not the kind of place to build a home.

There are no residents. Here, all conscious life
is in transit, neither here nor there, as we learn our exile
queuing behind our trolleys in single or double file,

craning our necks to the windows for the first chance to see
great machines fathom the clouds to open their alloyed bellies,
taking us from where we were to where we need to be.

Confession to the Southwest

Spread-eagled as the repentant thief upon the crucifix,
she indicates our nearest exits with an upturn of her wrists

and waits until each shutter opens and every groin is buckled
before she shuffles sternwards to her own dark cubicle

where she knows the build up as a pressure on her womb
more like a clutch of life inside than the prelude to orgasm,

as the braceletted planet tilts under the weight of Birmingham,
and even the atheists make the sign of the cross, an aluminium

angel scudding less than a mile high, where the heavens split
darkness from clouds: droplets from the glass: nails from her wrist.

Myrrh

If there's a didin tree upright on this stretch of coast,
I'll crack the silver bark to carve an eye on the wood
with a chit of wax-paper to gather the gummy crust.

Suspended in oil, it makes a liniment for the dead.
Scattering it on embers and letting the smoke brush
on a swollen vulva helps bring on the flow of blood.

Tonight the sky's ablaze with a streak of cosmic dust.
Somewhere in the rubble a woman stares overhead
with starlight on her womb. She's not expecting us.

The Hour Star

A lozenge for eternal life made of crushed jade and mercury
turned First Emperor Ying Zheng's blood the shade of mercury.

He survived the blind minstrel and Jianli's knife in the map case,
but died as the lining of his stomach became inlaid with mercury.

As did the bluefin tuna of Minamata who gorged their stomachs grey
on smaller fish that swam where pipes filled the bay with mercury.

Local cats danced to their deaths. Crows fell and algae decayed.
Children coughed softly into hankies stained with mercury.

Before the tally of the bodies, thermometers were felt to shake
within their mouths, dowsing the sympathetic trace of mercury.

Ying Zheng's tomb lies unopened. Rivers of quicksilver, it is said,
meet in the central darkness in an unshimmered lake of mercury.

The ceiling is hung with a map of heaven rendered in polished jade.
The smallest is Ch'en-Hsing, the Hour Star, one name for Mercury.

A perfect sphere, inedible. Even if the metal finds its place
within our bellies, nothing will perturb the face of Mercury.

A Bird in the Hand

Unravel the future from the steel inches of the bird gutter
twisted three times and pulled from the herring gull's hole

to loosen the kidneys from the fleshier part of the soul
and unloop grey curls of intestine from the oversized liver,

working your end off the hook – of course it is cancer –
inked where the airsacs have torn from the gull's hollow bones

your career like a glyph worried onto the round gizzard stones,
quartz pebbles that hail from Oostende. Go ahead. Dip a finger.

Star Matter

Orion's plump root hangs beside the jogger's wet reflection,
or hung this way eight hundred years ago, when the photons

rattled aeons from the core through the debris of stars
still spinning in the wake of a nova in the Crab Nebula,

to touch a carapace of eggs crunched under the jogger's foot.
He comes to rest, clutching his naked knees, his breath and fat

back steaming. Wet eyeballs flicker over what he stepped on.
Keys are bunched between his fingers as a rudimentary weapon,

in case a dog comes at him. He lets the lactic acid gather
like a ball of ethers in his throat as he stoops to deliver

a nebula to the silenced crab. Perhaps he is star-matter,
a brief collision of waves and particles, as the sea water

takes the matter back into itself, and his reflection
resumes position on the sand by the swung root of Orion.

Lega' Ten'er

Tho ye may scratch the ee ou a the English Queen,
wee man, diggin yir compass inta thon spodgy cheek,

doan think yiv haff a hope ti bline her. An wha, ye niver
got yir twa pack a Meanies afore yir break, an aftir,

yir wan in the Shanty Mobile refuse ye a single Benson.
Yer money's here ti stay. Go an; an ye tik tae spinnen

her aa across the disk, an watch the licht come skitten
through her perfick steely ball; but doon she flattens,

ye'll find her keekin up at ye. An scrape awaa,
yir naim inti the shilter, whativer, up the 'Ra,

but mind ye blow the pint aff uv her silver idge.
She'll no be shucked up by a wain's no privilidged.

Ye mind tha trick ye lick the back and press her agin
the fuirheid? An niver mind the tist uv blud, the porsin

uv muir'n a hunder thumbs. Ye'll feel her mark be stain
upon yir skin till lang after it gang. Wee man.

Vertigo on the Glenshane Pass

I was not bothered by the stitching under your eye
until we reached the plateau and you fell in the heather
where a barbed wire fence covered a seam in the sky,

stitching the clods of earth and the clouds together
as if it would take no more than a turn of the wind
to unthread each half and lift one clean of the other,

shearing the sky to a darkness that would never end,
with one of us tumbling upwards in perpetual freefall
the other strung on a barbed knot of steel by one hand,

all life on the globe scabbing over like a loose eyeball
unmoored on a nerve and dulling to cataracts slowly,
the dry world darkening, fences and heather and all.

Jupiter

Your mouth tugs on the cigar hooked to the side of your head,
as your fishing rod arches like a thunderbolt over Pierhead.

Two lungfuls split a cloud of smoke and rub the halves together,
just as the heavens break their vows of silence overhead.

The trout pulls down, burping excess gasses from his bladder,
tearing from the skyward tug for the coolness under his head.

I am kneeling on the pier, off my head on smoke and beer,
dry heaving as the rain falls hard on my unsheltered head.

I could breath more easily in the red spot of Jupiter
where the gas giant gathers in a cyclonic thunderhead.

Here the planet has earned its name: *Dieu-Pater, Thunderfinger,*
He who Rapes with Swan's Wings, Bull Fucker, the Fatherhead.

He who held the last Telchines of Rhodes beneath the water
only pausing when each head bobbed against another head.

When I am at myself, you have unzipped the air bladder
from the trout like red wind-chimes from its severed head.

There is a red spot on your coat, below your heart, just over
your lungs. My legs are shaking. Pass a cigar to clear my head.

Flood Warning

Should your car give up on the flooded byewash
do not open your window. Turn off the headlights
and watch the dead limp down from Creggan Heights
sloshing their finery through the barium overwash.
Those with cracked limbs will crawl as others hold
barbed wire for their passage. Sandbags are useless;
without knocking, they will enter their former houses,
unsettling your plasma screens and arranging photos
throughout the blackouts. Do not be alarmed.
Should you see someone you recognise, refrain
from calling their name and showing your position.
Reports have shown more people in floods are harmed
by open manholes than toothmarks in the brain,
but safety first. Do not alert your children.

The First of February

When even the sand sits under a thin plane of ice,
it's easy to be caught off guard by a seagull's skeleton.

It could be our first case of bird flu, or the cold and old age,
fed it to the fish and washed it up here by the stones.

Knots of bone twisted together like the crossing of rushes
woven by Brigid at the foot of her chieftain's deathbed,

soothing the ills of his body, and freeing his soul
to skit off the coast and pat its wet feet on the waves.

★

In Faughart, her shrine has stones for a number of ailments.
A back stone, a stone for the stomach and one for the head.

By a stream, the knee stone is scored with a double hollow,
holes for a pilgrim to kneel in and pray for his joints.

The eye can be cured by a shallow in the seat of the back stone.
No matter the month, it is said, this rock will hold water.

One February, I will watch the blind pilgrims in Faughart
rubbing the ice to rinse out the cups of their eyes.

★

Lambing season had caught us, alone on the farm.
You watched me from the doorway of the night,

tucking my forefinger into the mouth of each lamb,
checking the warmth of the spittle under their tongues.

Clammy was bad; but their spit was warm and milky
and none of them died. We climbed the hay together

thinking to take our chance and roll in it,
but the answer to every advance was the steam in our breath.

★

Frozen grasses and the frozen branches of trees
line the tracks of the trainline from Dundalk to Newry.

Another ribboned menu for our reception
offers variations of fowl and racks of lamb.

White bushes pass by the window. All these white leaflets
might serve just as well for one sacrament as another.

When we get married, let it not be in February.
Let us hold on for one of the warmer months.

Star of the Sea

Full of the slow interplanetary grace of green plankton
that blooms in the aerial photographs taken each May,
your downturned face appearing just off the Meath coast,
praise be. And praise for all these, the fruits of your womb,
festered in caverns and fed on by leather-backed turtles,
lumpfish snapping medusae through stalks in the biomass,
the gravel beds swollen with dark populations of copepods;
an abundance of larvae and brill, and fully grown whiting
dropped from the nets to feed the cowled seals of Howth Bay.
Deliver unto us a shark's corpse for the mouth of the Nanny,
whipped by the sewage, foaming at each crook of the bank,
where mattress springs rust in the bracken, clotted with weed,
and algae piles up on the desiccated scallops and starfish.
Lead us to accept that the surplus of life can mean death,
as the unrestrained growth in our cells develops to cancer;
and as isotopes blow to the clouds drifting in from the east
to dislocate ions in the rain that falls over your depths,
pray for us. Pray for us now and at the hour of our death.

Thirteen Foot by Six

This is our yard. No kittens drowned in the coalbucket,
though nappies freeze in winter and the frogs get ossified
in coaldust. The sheets are hung to dry in double lines,
making the wind more audible as the space becomes
a damp offstage to the house. Blackberries are banned,
as is frogspawn and later, fagbutts, although she coughs
each morning in, no matter whose windows are opened.
There is no problem with shifting stones to torture woodlice
if you leave the strawberry beneath the ferns untouched.
Noonish, get the short-haired brush to scrub the mulch
out of the concrete ridges around the wheeliebin.
Above the drain is where we leave her cross when time
has come to hide the plastic swords. This is our yard.

On the Sudden Passing of a Crow

Limbo beneath the wet bed-sheets drawn on the wind
with nothing above but a thin band of sky, wrapped in

the flags of our housekeeping, clean of our hair and the stains
of our sleep, as they bluster about you in three separate planes

of whiteness, bare as your unbaptised siblings in their limbo
of unwritten names, where each vowel is hollow, as hollow

in the book of the sky as the dent of a head on a pillow,
and would be as silent except for the squawk of a crow

opening now – don't crick your neck – like a handprint
of charcoal, mawkish, inelegant, marking her passing.

Eat the Turf

Whiskey alone will not flush these fibres. Like the magpie
who eats everything, you will need a few mouthfuls of water,
while your mother bends over the sink, rinsing her teeth,

but when the turf eats her, she can claim her citizenship
by the walnut of Ireland within her, woody with grit,
beneath the wet grass and the magpie who eats everything.

Small Explosions

for Nia and Conor

Don't bother acting the maggot in the house of the dead.
Go soak the yard with coke and mentos bombs instead.

Let the brown plumes splatter droplets on your face
as the moon rolls like a mint in the dark cola of space.

Perhaps a soul can pause its long trek in the moondust,
turning ankle-deep to glimpse back down upon us.

So come and splash the concrete in the cooling dark
before she fizzles out in the space between the stars.

Requiem for a Requiem Shark

The necropsy left no doubt; this was a miracle of death.
Unpeeled from her womb lay the body of the christpup,

teeth crusting out its mouth, with a dorsal fin the breadth
of a thumbnail, tipped in black. The finprint of its makeup,

said Dr. Chapman, proved the non-existence of a father.
Angelsharks burrowed deeper into the ocean bottom.

There was no rising afterwards. Lights above the water
were only torches held by men from the aquarium.

Vuningoma's Funeral

As they all sat crowded
under the shade of the acacia,
one child fumbled
at the breast of its mother

who undid her shirt
and offered herself
to the small brown hands
of the child, who did not heed

the flies on the brown skin
or the veins beneath it.
As the priest stood above
and said his mass

the breast began
to hang more thinly,
so the child moved over
to bare the other.

Heraclites Bathes at Kivu

Charlotte lost her glasses, skinny dipping; so he duckdives through the water,
scraping trails through leaves and lakemud, then surfacing to bare his palms,

near where she stands, blinking, from the pier. The world just cups this calm,
but aches to mesh the whole reflected heavens with raindrops cast like gravel,

to soak the linked canoes, or shift the gas that cramps its molten bowels,
huge methane clouds that boil from silence to sink the boats and skin and crows.

This lake has swallowed everything at some point. Her words are swallowed,
they couldn't be that far out, as he upends himself out past the marker bottles;

his gaze is gulped down in the deepening blues. But as the evening settles,
he'll take the shore and towel off, and watch the air chill in the rain.

Tomorrow, or when she's dead, there may be time to trawl the lake again,
but he'll not find her glasses. Children may limp from Goma with new sandals,

the lake bed will hide beneath great balls of frozen magma, and spectacles
such as these get trapped forever as fossils, despite the feeder rivers.

The Stand-Up Comic as the Letter C

The curl of a snail or an ear at a debate over water charges,
the eyelash on the pale of an envelope scored with two addresses,
the snapped ring of Play-Doh you offered a cousin at lunchtime

or your first note on piano? No tadpole is this delicate.
Perhaps the larval mosquito, bobbing in the village cistern,
that slops into the basin used to wash your clothes and face?

Nothing is funny as it used to be, except for the man as corrupt
as a corrupted hard-drive. And the laughless ghosts of pirates
in their hard-bellied boats, sipping rum to the wet edge of earth.

Tourists at S. 21

Above the skinless photo a housemartin has made its nest,
from which the noise is not unlike the scratch of pencil-tips.
Droppings line the halls to nineteen other silenced classrooms.

Kelly wets her fingers and dabs some water on her neck,
standing before a cartoon with an X drawn on its lips,
outside the room with photos of the faces of the victims.

The Salt Harvest

Scald bikinis left hanging on the rail, and wind the bedclothes
round sticks in laundry vats to stew the juices from the linen.
Even the towels hold traces of their body salts. We'll mop
the rest from deckchairs, the rim of an abandoned margarita,
their dinnerplates. Evaporate the sludge for the residue.

Scrape out the pots and crush the piles into rough mounds, like snow,
carving out calves and buttocks as one might palm a soldier's salary,
close enough to hear her breathe as she blinks back over Sodom.
You know what happened to her daughters? The rain shall crumble her
as honeymooners watch the monsoon from their balconies.

Banana Woman

Under the rattling firmament of leaves,
the purple head of the feathered serpent
yawns for Eve to pluck one tooth. Peeled,

it bears the paleness of a taxman, a new scent
pulped against her tongue to a sugared paste,
announcing that boys will fly, that continents

will soon rule their economies by taste,
green fingers clutched like stowaways as shipments
curve around the necks of nations. Great Quetzal

nods in wisdom, as panting down the path
the Grey God meets her fallen skin and tumbles
arse over face. Eve turns on him, and laughs.

German Names for Birds

Der Habicht und der Turmfalke: der Specht,
die Blaumeise. Birds speak the slipsoft voices
of the valley. They know the moods of rock,
its depth, its infertility.

Your grandparents slept in this wooden house,
when summer freed them from his pharmacy
in Celle. They knew each one by song alone;
but after storms, the birds were speechless

clutching wet boughs along the wooded cuffs
of granite. So they stand now, like feathered bottles
of pills and purgatives; shelved contraceptives;
toxic, dark-eyed, motionless.

A Period of Ellipsis

Wine has been spilt, and Burgundy stains dry on our lips, as
we pause our dispute and follow a marauding caravan of ants
connecting our table to their swollen nest in a trail of ellipsis.

The sun and moon and the earth line up as the planet turns silent
but for the click of these mandible kisses passing nectar in sips as
the queen swells into her pods where even the dust is pregnant,

but I could trace a line connecting your hips to your solar plexus
with no bumps or dips. The moon swells through the sun aslant
reaching suspension point with a blink as the daylight eclipses.

Osiris and the Prague Flood

Watching the fertile but flat and watery landscape passing –
I thought of how we had laughed bewildered as teenagers
returning from a night of wine with Christians – at how
they could smile at us but know us damned forever –
in a river of fire with pagans forever mute to God –
and now that my relationship had ended – the bad sex
and the lack of sex – the meals where both of us wished
to be sat at other tables – eat from lives not yet our own –

and coming to see you had been a part of that – escape –
not seen since I'd left with two Czech girls – they camped
with me beside a river – past tragic tussles in a two man tent –
but meeting you in *Pizza Ovenecka* – with your young wife –
so beautiful and new and Catholic – and you with God
now finally – the wine tasted wrong or odd and we knew –
something was amiss – was it the weather of those days –
or would the blood of Christ be stale till I had left you –

and the television showed the national signs of this unrest –
the flood was moving down towards the city – small towns
allowed their banks to break to stop the flow – it did not stop –
old women lifted by helicopter from the roofs of houses –
men boating down the streets they'd always lived in –
and the bars we went to in the pauses – leaving your wife
to wrap up blankets for the council – were empty –
and my book of poems was nearly empty – and our talk –

as the city filled to the brim with water – overspill –
in the darkness on the Charles Bridge – jazz bands replaced
by rain and the flash of sirens – the stories – the elephant
shot in his cage – the overwash of chemicals – the priest
who said his mass despite the kneehigh depth of water –
the ten-thousand-dollar chair swept from the gallery
like so much jetsam – the seal that left the zoo – escaped –
to end up poisoned when the Voltova became the Elba –

how silt would end up thick across the cobbles – the stains
on buildings – the cars now washed away – the grubby silence
that would haunt the city – and as we stood in darkness –
sharing an umbrella with your sister – I knew I could not
place my hand on hers – thinking of Osiris far from home –
watching the flooding of the Nile without his penis –
and you looking at me through the rain – as if all my teeth
had fallen out – and I was calling out for this destruction.

Frog

is the taste of oxides through the skin.
Winter as a buried square of oak.
Limbless dreams of bites at wavering algae.
Rare wakeful blinks onto brown films of moisture.
Slow pulse; the weighted world a rootful murmur.
Spring a tingled ooze of warmth in threetoes,
memories. Awareness, nosing earth
to wind electrified with the pull to feed.

Horror as a skyfall feathersweep.
Roar of lights on tarmac. Wellyboots,
sloshing palmfuls of spawn destined to sour.
The squeal of cousins rattled in fingercages.
Traces of opened bodies. Freeze at horror;
stalks make cover, soil is like-my-colour,
leaves my-shape. Sweat when it gets close;
leap is panic, leap is fling-of-flesh.

The wind is tug of moist hooks through our pores.
This journeylife. The need for other places,
ratless waters, bog of nightsongs, marsh
of grabbing skinbirth. Smelling the horizon,
gone to them. Hide under things, and watch.
My tongue is half-my-gaze, the flies are food
gripped. This travel on roughbelly concrete,
groundhug mud. We march, and taste the air.

Crocus, column; break, murder, walk;
church, meagre, brick; walk, squad;
scrotum, squad; root, shrub, stench;
wench, bottom, relish; marriage, chorus;
rummage, wench, wrench; felch, squirt;
breach, retch. Learn the song in belchnotes
and soft farting. Brood, grass, squad;
murder, blemish. Blood. Chorus. Walk.

Danger and leaves and no two close, and sing.
When she is there, saddle her thrust, her bridge,
and stirrup and buckle. Aware of the comet above
burning skin, bursting a nibble at clouds,
flaring through your frogsoul as you spurt.
Then break, to hold the soil. Winter is soon
and you have memories. The comet will come
and this will be again. But first the winter.

The Grilse at Drogheda

Boynewater flushes salt from gills back in the run of sacfries.
Smelling orange in her redd, he breaches the walls of the clutch
and shunts his sudden gutful of light in clouds onto the pebbles.

Dipping the air, he scoots his gaze beyond the Ottoman ships
to bright pricks in the darkwater behind their veil of spunk.
Empty now. When the spawn has eyed he will be belly up.

Jaws Zero

I will go for a swim. I will ignore the shark warnings,
though the woman in the bandana should scream at me;
I will pass the mill of panicked children to the water.

I will unclothe myself beneath a damp towel on the rocks,
feeling my shorts rub sand into my buttocks. I will watch
for the shark-fin, past the crowded beach to the horizon,

and will not be deterred. As I weave through tumbled lilos,
dilapidated sandcastles, the mothers bent over and crying,
my feet will crunch the thick shells; my chest meet wind,

for I will go swimming today. The scuffled sand underfoot,
even the atheist footprints of Michael Palin, now lost at sea,
will not distract me; I will stand with cut rools and lengths

of seaweed looped and sucking around my numbing ankles.
The far slate-blue, the olive-green, the nearer sandy-green,
the interference of white that tubes and falters in its motion,

the aching muscles and the taste of salt. I will go swimming,
where the coldness of my head breaks through in hard thumps,
and the hidden scrapes of rock give way to spastic kicking,

where my limbs grow swollen and useless, the air comes short,
and nothing underscreen is tempted to nip my senseless calves;
with no blood frothing, and no-one to watch me from the shore.

Extra Terrestrial

How much snow will it take to sink Bolzano?
The ectoplasm unravels through his nose
leaving the earth in coils of cigar smoke.

Like a swollen finger, an *Agio* dips its glow
and hisses out. Now he will never know
how much snow it will take to sink Bolzano,

even as the greyed-out vision of his soul
snags on the clouds in thin pneumatic ropes
leaving the earth in coils of cigar smoke.

A boy has pressed his face to a plane window.
Dear Eliot, come now, give up the ghost.
See how much snow is falling on Bolzano.

His four squat lumps of flesh have been laid low,
more lumber in the lumber yard. Gone cold.
He's left the earth in coils of cigar smoke,

so turn back at Brescia airport. Go. Phone home.
He has taken the route no bicycle can follow.
Look how much snow it took to sink Bolzano.
Leave him to the earth and cigar smoke.

No Smoking Beyond This Point

Breath being one mode of existence of my body,
I light a cigar on the platform, imagining my lungs
voluminous as the curing barns of Vinales Valley,

where seco, then viso and then ligero leaves are strung
hoisted on wire across the wooden ribs of the ceiling,
a lettuce browning and fluted like organ-pipes, hung

for a gestation of six weeks in their thick ammonial stink
until men layer a mattress of all the reshuffled sheaves,
to rot in warm precision. The tobacco rollers' fingers

darken as they bind each cylinder of weeds
by which I inhale some god or other through the fumes,
and exhale myself over the trains and the sign before me.

No smoking beyond this point. The world is split in two,
with you on the side where children breathe as restfully
as oxen, train-tracks stretching like decades ahead of you.

The Last High King of Ireland

No elephants in the elephant house. This pied bird
lifts from grubbed straw to loosen his throat in the rain,
as the lining of clouds smashes onto the marmot enclosure,
and buckles on fishy concrete. He is barking for scales
where *srebro* is silver and *ostrze* a thin blade in his gums
to cut out the clot of dark blood coiling under his tongue
like the sins of a Scotsman. *Craic*, calls the magpie, *crack*.

The Naming of the Rat

Foreigner. Coiled on stones, fur-thorned and black
on bald skin, like His crown, staring from Antrim's shore
over the Scottish sea-world. Who dared the hobbled swim

once the frozen saltbridges had melted. Or huddled
in the wooden core of longboats, hushed, recoiling
at the seal-clad shins in *brøkke*. To parleyed nobles,

you shall be *Francach*, French one; and to their servants,
your name the hiss of boiling water poured in holes,
till monks close you in pages. *Rattus Norwegicus.*

Clutch four pink fingers to the rock. There's eating here.
And not till the eleventh raid, within a burnt church,
nested in a native's ribcage dense with grasses,

five suckling polyps of youth blind at your thinning teats,
shall Christ walk to you, past the grey-haired scavengers
collecting bits of metal from the freshest corpses.

His hand inside to touch you, matted organ. *You too
are mine; but every night shall be a night of long knives.
They will train dogs to snap the spines of little ones,*

*make poison, snares of steel. Though you hide in crisp-bags,
run through streams of shit, clutch to corner-rubbish,
they shall hunt you. Whenever their children wail with jaundice,*

*wander with eyes like holes, you will be blamed by them.
And crucified, injected, smothered, drawn and quartered.
But still, I ask you, never be more than ten rat-lengths*

from each. Eat what they leave, and learn to creep. Stay close.
Red eyes of the white rats, black eyes of the brown
still locked behind the birth-swelling of lids, shall nuzzle

into His skin, lick blood trickling from His palm wounds;
sky gaze turned to the mewling runt. *Even you,
the littlest of all. I call you Sailor's Warning.*

Pissabed

A thousand stomata swell their lips to our wet matins.
Each silent nova throws its rags above Gethsemane,
rooting where dogs have pissed and in the holy garden.
Gruff Christ on rising does not have the palms to shield
His gaze from all this fruitfulness. He blesses the land,
and blesses all the weeds but those with lion's teeth.

Calypso on the Third Day

The sea churns with seersucker and red ware.
As he withdraws, the heavens batter the glass.
I'd tell him that sugar wrack and witches' hair
drag one new face each month below the kelp
but he's off, shouldering out in the spitting air
to wear the southern sea-palm and the seabelt
like a devil's apron. Black tang and pigweed
poke through his fingers as he scrubs himself,
clumps of sea-otter's cabbage and broadleaf.
The taste of twisted wrack crushed on the lips,
is part the final sluice a drowned man breathes,
and part his own salt puddled between my hips.
He'll stumble back like Jesus in his goggles,
blinking in this world's light, limbs gone limp
as fingertang and as numb as the sea girdles
he'll have me peel in ribbons from his back,
when he rises again on my belly, unpalatable
as shotgun kelp and slick as bladderwrack.

1054

The papal throne is empty: no more shall Constantinople sit with Rome,
and in Rossdalla, the earth is stripped of cattle and the roots of trees
are pulled skyward through a blackened tower of air the like unseen,
and the only brightness is the new body burning in the ring of Taurus
even through daylight. This to the east, by the ink of Wei-te's brushes,
and west to Chaco Canyon, where the last Anasazi starman hacks
a hand, a crescent moon and a blistered ball onto the lip of rock,
before returning to his orange city in the lap of the broken earth
after what solace lies in spirits or women. Let us take each other
now upon our knees like animals to dull the closing boom.

Et in Mosnia Ego

Treble clefs and figures of eight, the doughnut, ampersands
free-wheeled on Mosney Beach beneath a snow that would not settle
watched only by the damp cavities of a beached Renault.

Uzbekistan and its trifold flag were scrawled in sand
although no gods or gulls dropped from the clouds to read it.
Inland, a steel fence rattled. We climbed out of the wind,

tearing lines back through the streams that fed the rising tide
until the bonnet dipped. Your awful noises cramped my stomach
as the salty gush rose to the dashboard; you clambered past me

out of our tiny cube of light that cast great whirling cones
into the dusk. Somewhere along the way, we'd missed the signs
and ended here, upon our knees, clawing the freezing sand.

134340 Pluto

Even a cartoon dog would be muzzled out here
where the planet is dwarved below the asteroid belt.
There are no names when you get this far from the sun
to imprint a feature against the tundra of methane.

The planet is just another dwarf in the asteroid belt.
Even if the rings of plutonium fused in our bombs
could hollow a hot lake into this tundra of methane
nothing would put an end to the perpetual winter.

Neither the dense metal rings we fuse in our bombs
nor a post-holocaustal nymph rising up from the wastes
could herald the end of this perpetual nuclear winter
and mutate our cells to a shape that is liveable here.

Expect no gaunt women rising from the wastes.
If you find a broken husband eyeballing the sky,
praying for her cells to somehow grow liveable here,
tell him to roll down onto his side and lie still.

For every broken husband must eyeball the sky,
when he finds there are no names this far from the sun.
Now turn on your side. Roll over, boy, and lie still.
Even the cartoon dogs must get muzzled out here.

Revenge of the Crabmonsters

After Lawrence Raab; for Colm and Fiona

1.
Crabmeat sizzles upon a pockmarked platter,
and your tits look cracking. I drain your glass,
light cracking the molecules of the water,
and chuck a discreet fiver to the waiter
just as you tumble heavily on your ass.

2.
Like crabmeat sizzling under its pockmarked platter,
spongy flesh ran through you. One of the cancers.
You took each drink they gave you, and did not ask
what light had cracked the molecules in the water.

3.
You poke for new growth where the skin is tender.
I hear your brain even when your face is downcast
like crabmeat sizzling under a pockmarked platter.
One day you'll get a bruise and there'll be laughter
instead of this slow probing of your crevasse.

4.
Lightning cracks the molecules through the water.
I scan the waves for the shadow of giant pincers,
straining my ears as I get smashed on our terrace
for crabmeat sizzling under a pockmarked platter,
or the light crackle of molecules beneath the water.

Martin Healy's War on God and Ireland

When I think of how windfarms form scything crucifixes on the horizon, with Jesus and His thieves cutting their arms through the air, with a deeply pervasive thwum-thwum-thwum that could be the swishing heartbeat of air,

and how Martin Healy was aware of them always as a curse on the land, as he carried his photos from house to bleak house along the cut of the coast, saying *this is the country we once had, here from the beach, and here from the mountains,* waving a brinedamp petition on windfarms,

and how the air blown from hymns came half-hissed from his lips every Sunday, except for the Christmas he stayed up with us and after a fair few hot whiskeys, air sung from his lungs like the spirit in *spiritus,* the breath of his body now left him,

and of the air's sudden change of direction tossing the leaves round the yard of his house, or in the lungs of the man on the moor who finds that the hills of his youth are now steeper, and wheezes the climb up the hills, cursing his God and his land and the change in himself,

or in the change of the breeze that took Martin's ashes, tossing them round us before Malin Beach where he'd asked they be spread, and we stood there grey-faced, looking ashen, some knowing we might want to cry each Ash Wednesday from now, and each time we saw the burnt wisps of a newspaper torn from a late autumn bonfire, wiping our faces in the walk to our cars by the ditches,

and how the ashes not caught in our hair or the grass of those fields, what survived the broad slice of revenge meted out by the white metal windmills he'd hated so long, was caught in the gulf stream, swept off the Atlantic, up towards Iona,

long after Columb Cille sailed a small wooden curragh up there, flee-
ing the barbarous practice the heathens still kept of burning their
dead, but leaving behind new stone crosses in fresh-planted grave-
yards, with limbs that were joined by a circle, as if limestone could
capture a motion,

and perhaps air could whistle through the gaps in the rock, only
heard when a monk wandered touchnear at night, unable to sleep on
his rough haycloth bed; and what the words of the gaps might sound
like to a monk late at night, covered or uncovered by small dustmotes
and ash as the tribes burnt their dead in the dark;

when I think of all this, it occurs to me that Martin has gone with
all the dead sparrows from the base of each windmill to challenge the
saint in Iona; but Columb will place these small corpsetwists of birds
round the roots of his letters, as a gloss to the T in the Trinity, or
interweaving the crux of the K in the Kingdom of God on the
island,

and Martin must come to his mountains where the three arms of
Christ keep him walking all night with no peace but the thwum of
the windfarms and crosses that Columb escaped, lone in a land
cursed by Christ and the saints and the deep Godly throttle of air.

An Ethical Taxonomy of Cordyceps

Cordyceps Militaris

Consider the fungus that sprouts from infected larva
erecting itself in the wetlands and shuck of Armagh,
parting the heather with the end of pale orange limb
with the same silent innocence as a melanoma.

Cordyceps Miryensis

The fruiting stroma will only breach the casing
when the downy mycelia has completed the invasion
ultimately penetrating the brain and the vital organs
in an almost perfect process of mummification.

Cordyceps Ochraceostromata

Is it more wonderful that the brain of a pupa
may sprout fungal growth, or that an older man
may eat of the fungus to feel the intemperate flush
of Qi disturb the unfurling cocoon of his gonads?

Cordyceps Sinensis

Tibetan ghost moths infused with the fruiting fungus
must be boiled in the gutted cavity of a duck carcass,
ensuring the patient takes both the flesh and the broth.
In this way we keep our Emperors among us.

Cordyceps Sobolifera

Consider instead the Emperor slack in his sack–cloth,
watching the patterns made by uninfected moths
as they bother his lamplight. Such life is untenable.
What can a nation gain from an old man's sloth?

Cordyceps Unilateralis

John the Baptist might offer the loosest of parables
for an ant cast from the borders of what is acceptable.
Driven on high by the growth in its brain, it crucifies
itself to the wood, with an awful wrenching of mandibles.

Cordyceps Washingtonensis

The white fungal tip exiting the head as it dies
breathes out tongues of spores, scattering quietly
as a dream of the second coming, coming all over
the bright and the beautiful under the canopy.

Taking Names

Overhead, iron sheets touch the deafening batter of rainfall.
Your speechless lips, and your face in its dull film of water,
are as cold as the wet in our clothes. Eyes to the tide,
now eating the damp names of children who ran to their cars.
Our view interrupted by thick boles of wood and rainwater

on what we thought was Stragill. The sign has been clipped,
neatly torn by the Bradleys who stood to their thighs in the nettles,
twisting steel sinews and working the hacksaw blade warm,
aluminium a euro a yard. Or maybe the Keaveneys.
The dark squall responds to each fresh act of negative baptism.

A Boiled Egg

One nubbed ovoid of protein is the perfect snack,
boiled and peeled for a wonky planet of albumen.
I dislocate my jaw, flip-topping my head as far back

as when I raspberried love songs onto your abdomen,
slabbering over our deaf unborn. Pointless, although
her fingers were not unlike the fingers of those children

who broke from hawking bracelets to let duck embryos
slop from the ends of chopsticks back into the damp
vegetable mash that simmered in the communal bowl

on one beach in Cambodia. There is almost a lump
at the back of my throat as my brainshell starts to crack.
There goes the hollow throughline of my jaw. Chomp.

Arena

Spanish sand, or Ceasar's bloodsports? Life, thrown from men in ropes,
could whip the ground in beads, and dry in clumps; easily shovelled
or tilled into the darkness underneath. Even when Androcles
plucked the thorn, a faint discolouration marked the instep
of every sixth print trailing from the crowd. Such weighty creatures,

unlike somebody's dachshund that shudders turds inside a tyre
half-up the dune, and sniffs at broken bottles that once were sand,
and unto which they have returned. The spiky grass
stings like murder on the ankles, as I watch a couple pass
into the distance. When the coast is clear, I'll spill my own libations.

Hibernation of the Canals

after Patrick McGuinness

*To our eventual descendants life on Mars will no longer be
something to scan and interpret ... The drying up of the planet
is certain to proceed until its surface can support no life at all.*
— Percival Lowell, Mars as Abode of Life

Children barely disturbed the air as they lay down and imploded.

The posters said *Head North*. I could not raise you from your bed.

You claimed you had seen a planet in the heavens blue with water.

I gnawed a crack into my tongue for a coppery tang of moisture.

The high street was silent but for the ticking of a bicycle.

Clothes gathered in a doorway where the few last dogs were huddled.

A set of footprints in the canal bed came to a sudden stop.

Fences divided the soil. The soil was cracked in hexagons.

I found a teepee made from orchid sacks, brimming with shoes.

When Phobos left the sky, Deimos rose like a molar tooth.

My own teeth crumbled. I had to finger the dust out of my gums

I could not tell the wind on the Phison from the ache in my
                                            diaphragm.

Will the desert keep its name when the last prints are gone?

Dustclouds the size of baobabs are mounting on the horizon.

Where I touch the world I leave the same powder as a moth.

I woke last night to feel sharp crystals fuzzing on the rock.

A scaffolding has ripped a furrow through the ground to ice.

White mountains shatter against the red dawn. I am terrified.

The Martians

They had already landed
        and learned how you bleed
                when the toad in your hands
pushed through your fingers
        and left your palm branded
                as the squeals of the thing,
thick with mortal juice,
        claimed our atmosphere thin.
                There might have been truce
if you hadn't turned back
        and pushed through the bushes
                on the backyard path
where the future descended
        as you rolled in the grass
                like a saucer descending
to circle the crops.
        It has come to an end.
                The bedsheets are sodden
with blood and your wife
        has stopped calling for God.
                This is the new life
forcing its slick curls
        part mucous, part light,
                through a gap between worlds
with its rage undiminished
        and the face of a girl.
                The old world is finished
and you served as a breeder.
        Your feel your palms twitch.
                Take her to your leader.

The Long Horizon

When all has been said and done and what remains is submergence
our bookshelves mulched and cathode ray tubes cracked under pressure

and a coelacanth noses our skulls on the carpet as it gums the last fibres,
the freezer aclick with live crabs and the windows gone back into sand,

as an octopus wraps itself round the steering wheel of our van
and thrusts out great billows of rust where the light fathoms slowly

over a copse of dead oaks given up to the brown limbs of algae,
and the horse in its trap is hollowed by seahorses into an ornament

having waited too long for an ark, and dust rolls through radio silence
reflected from satellites forever in orbit with no landing signal

and the waves have nowhere to crash except for the odd mountain steeple
where the last nesting gulls batter and fry as the lightning grounds

and there are no more words for rain when the only recognisable sound
is the sounding of bells slower than whalesong as the tides keep rising

with floating canopies of corpses that give up their gas and then sink
past the curious mouths of fish on the long drop back to the cities

and the leviathan rolls in Hyde Park beneath a waterlogged sky
and jellyfish parachute over Tokyo in the wartime flash of an eel,

tell me whose fingers will indent our daughter's ribs as her heels
dance the mad dance of the Jesus Christ lizard, hurdling the troughs

and the waves in the settling night, down onto her ramshackle cot
with two handfuls of sushi? Who will praise her diligence?

Felix, Bene Futuis

Now that your milk-soaked pyjamas are cast
onto the floor, the child asleep at last,
I gorge myself on great palmfuls of breast,
not thinking of the burial mounds of Meath
nor even of Cleopatra's milky baths
but a brothel a thousand years under the ash
in Pompeii, at the juncture of two alleys,
where a fresco bares the *fiilatris*, Myrtales
gorging on Felix astride her well decked pallet
softer than what survives her – the bare stone –
even as I blink beneath these new eruptions
of breastmilk pooling at our intersection.

Augury for Katja

Three digits stretched to the tips of the herring gull
will open the globe of the air. Look how his head lifts,
divining your approach from the guts of a razor clam,
and the stunted crease of your palms – you can't touch this –
as he hunches to embrace one more day with his belly-down
leaving a shadow I guess we will mimic by torchlight.

The Ripples of Saturn

You sit in my ripples as I bare your armpit
soaping the length of your clavicle slowly
your ribcage as tight as the meat of a rabbit,

like the meat of the rabbit that surpassed expectation,
tugged from her skin and cracked for the pot
caramelised a deep red with chillis and onion,

or the meat of the mad hinds hollowing Queensland,
undermining barnyards, graveyards and foundations
unsettling the carcasses like squat Sons of Man,

or the meat of an old buck with chemical burns,
his foamed eyes outstaring the rifle as he bends
to unlatch his jaws on young huddles of fur,

and you scream as shampoo flushes the gullies
of your eyes, and I think of Goya's Saturn,
as I raise you like bread from my fat gravity.

Bird Strike

Blue eyes at the moment, but your resting colour is yet undefined

on our airport drive, as we unsettle a murder of rooks from the roadside.

Brown or rusted copper? You reach for their flight through the window

clutching and unclutching your hands as if groping through a
                                        feather pillow

to find the body of a bird. You are restless. You were restless last night,

and will suckle and struggle in take-off, new to both earache and flight,

until we are caught in the all-coloured unblinking eye of the sun.

I pray against bird strike. I have an idea why seagulls and pigeons

nosedive the engines, shredding steel fans with their hollow bird bones

lost in an instant of red mist to claim the airways for their own,

but I want you to live. I want you to defy me, bold and upright,

staring out from a torrent of feathers in the wake of a pillow fight,

brazen in your future. So I think of US Airways Flight 1549,

both engines snagging on snow geese on the take off for
                                        North Carolina,

as the pilot skimmed down on the icy Hudson where his passengers
                                        and crew

were lifted alive from the water. His eyes were a turbine of blues.

Acknowledgements

Some of these poems or versions of them appeared in the following magazines: *London Magazine; Poetry Ireland; Poetry London; Poetry Wales; Poetry Proper; Brand; Ulster Tatler; Trespass; Orbis.* A number of these poems were also anthologised in *NW14* (Granta) and *Incertus* (Netherlea Press), and some have been recorded for www.poetcasting.co.uk. Thanks are due to all editors and parties involved.

Thanks also to An Chomhairle Ealaíon for its generosity, helping me put this collection together.

I would also like to thank the following readers:
Miriam Gamble, Paul Maddern, Alex Wylie, Sinead Morrissey and Medbh McGuckian.

Lastly, thanks to Leonie, Katja and Roisín, for bearing with me. I love you all.